FREE YOUR SPIRIT, CHANGE YOUR LIFE

THE ULTIMATE WOMAN'S GUIDE TO REDISCOVER
YOUR PASSION & UNLEASH YOUR BRILLIANCE

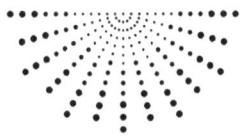

MARTHA MOORE

Copyright © 2017 by Martha Moore

All rights reserved.

No part of this book may be reproduced in any form or by any electronic or mechanical means, including information storage and retrieval systems, without written permission from the author, except for the use of brief quotations in a book review.

Published 2017 by Ingenium Books.

Surrey, B.C. Canada V3C 7S9

www.ingeniumbooks.com

ISBN Paperback: 978-0-9959346-7-2

ISBN Electronic book: 978-0-9959346-8-9

CONTENTS

Introduction	1
Section 1: Breaking Down Barriers	7
1. Is This All There Is?	9
2. Expectations: Internal and External	15
3. Career Burnout	21
4. Limiting Beliefs	25
Section 2: Baby Steps to Big Dreams	37
5. My Story	39
6. Being A Free Spirit	45
Section 3: Change Your Life, Create, and Commit	49
7. Be the Creator of Your Own Life	51
8. In The Flow	59
9. Dream Discovery	67
10. Unleash Your Free Spirit in Eight Weeks	75
Conclusion	87
Additional Resources	91
About the Author	95
End Notes	97

INTRODUCTION

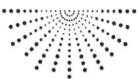

We all want passion. We want to feel passionate about our relationships, our careers, and most certainly our life. It's critical to our health and happiness. Yet it seems the older we get, the further this burning desire drifts from our lives.

What if I told you that by following a simple eight-week process you could rediscover your passion for life and unleash your free spirit? My techniques have helped more than a thousand satisfied clients reawaken their passion for life, find their dream jobs and careers, improve their health, and manifest more money. Their dreams have come true. And so can yours.

But first, you have to identify what isn't working in your life. Why are you feeling numb or dissatisfied with your life? Is it just a midlife crisis? Or, is it something more? Maybe you're suffering from career burnout or you're physically exhausted. Maybe you're in a relationship that has drained you of joy. Or perhaps it's not about rekindling your passion, but finally *finding* it.

I'm writing this book for you if you're a woman in that mid-life stage, between 35 and 64, and you've recently woken up and looked at your life, saying, 'What have I done with my life? What am I doing now? Where am I going?'

You've been doing what you saw your mom and dad do, whether it fits you or not. And your parents were doing what *their* parents did, and what society expected of them. No questions asked. Well, now it's time for you to start asking questions: 'Is this hamster wheel life I'm living right for me?' 'Maybe there's another way.' 'Is it too late to make the changes I want to make?'

I'm here to tell you that you don't have to stay on the hamster wheel anymore. There *is* another way and it is not too late to begin to pursue your dream life.

I want to share with you the free spirit formula that you can use to bring passion into your life and unleash your free spirit. But before we talk about how to find your passion, we need to understand how you lost it in the first place.

DOES THIS SOUND LIKE YOU?

You're exhausted physically, emotionally, and financially. You're stressed out and overwhelmed. You're anxious. You don't sleep well at night. You have health issues. You're taking medications for a number of stress-related diseases. You gain more weight every year. You struggle in your relationships.

You're quick to anger and easily frustrated. You dread Monday mornings and have trouble getting out of bed.

Just like Bill Murray's character in the movie *Groundhog Day*, you feel like you're repeating the same day over and over and over again. And things aren't changing. You're not changing. You know you are affecting your family, friends and co-workers because you're not happy. You want to change – but you don't know where to start.

Well, I do.

In this book, I will take you through my *Unleash Your Free Spirit: Change Your Life* step-by-step program to help you:

- target and identify the beliefs that are holding you back,
- get back in touch with the gifts and talents you had as a child,
- identify the patterns among the stumbling blocks you have experienced in your past,
- dream big,
- ignite your passion, and
- come up with a game plan to put all the pieces together.

Here are 10 critical keys to the free spirit formula that I will cover in detail in this book:

1. It's never too late to change and do what you love.
2. There are no overnight successes – you need to stick with it.

3. The process is simple. It's not easy, but it is very simple.
4. It begins with baby steps – and you build your dream, step by step.
5. You have to become 'selfish' – to put your oxygen mask on first. You are no good to anyone else if you aren't breathing.
6. There is no 'right' way. There is no one way to do it. Your way is the only one that matters. But you have to decide what your way is and stick with it.
7. It takes commitment, determination, perseverance, and courage.
8. Motivation is something that you have to work at – just like relationships, jobs, and anything in life that matters.
9. You must have a support team or cheerleading squad to help you stay on track, provide support, give feedback, and encourage you when you need it.
10. Abundance, freedom, joy, happiness, love: EVERYTHING lies within.

MY JOURNEY

On my journey to becoming a free-spirited woman, I travelled all over the world and within myself looking for answers. I challenged myself outside and in, facing some of my biggest fears and uncovering deep-seated limiting beliefs. I will share more of my story with you later in the book but I promise you, it's been a journey worth taking.

I can honestly say that I'm now living life my way. I have freedom and, for me, that is what's most important. And I'm going to keep living my life this way.

I want to help you change your life so you can live it the way that YOU want to live it, to move out of the frustration, hopelessness and hamster wheel experience that you are in right now. Then you can take what you have learned and be an example to your children, your partner, your family, your friends, your co-workers, and your colleagues. You can be the shining light that encourages them to move out of the fear and helplessness of their stuck lives into a place that is full of change, challenge, power, strength, courage, and interdependence. That's when you and those around you will make decisions – not from fear, but from a place of courage and the desire to live a free life; a life fulfilled by your own dreams and desires and not those of the culture and society that you live in.

Then you will truly be living the life of a free-spirited woman.

Are you ready? Time to free your spirit and let yourself soar!

SECTION 1: BREAKING DOWN BARRIERS

1
IS THIS ALL THERE IS?

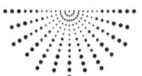

*A*s we move into our 40s and head toward retirement age, many of us start to look at our lives and wonder, 'What has happened to me? Why am I still in a job or career that I hate? Why am I still living in a house that has sucked the life out of me, financially and emotionally? What happened to the dreams I was so excited about when I was young?' These profound questions all converge into two universal questions that haunt most of us in modern society: 'Is this it? Is this all there is?' And then comes the realization that time is running out and this is indeed all we've got. In fact, we're probably more than halfway through this life.

THE WAYS WE LOSE OUR PASSION

In many societies, and the United States in particular, we don't really encourage change. We find safety in keeping things the same. When we teach children and young adults to learn a new skill, we tell them that this is what they should be doing for the rest of their working lives. And then when they retire, their choices are limited to playing golf or bridge or living in a retirement community. Not only do we strive to keep things the same in our day-to-day lives, we also have it drilled into our heads that part of the American dream is buying a house and that we should own our house for a long time, 30 to 40 years or longer. We are told by study after study that it is much cheaper to buy a house than to rent and that owning a house is a good investment. And we believe it, even when the numbers just don't add up.

I have a client who owns a home that she rents out. The home is worth a lot of money, which is fantastic. Right? And yet my client is unhappy. She wants to start a new business but doesn't have the money to do it. She frequently argues with her husband over their financial situation. The rental property is in another state and she has constant issues to address with maintenance, tenants, and the property manager. She is convinced that she needs to keep the rental property because it is her safety net, and yet, her whole situation is stressing her out and literally making her sick. The 'safety net' has become the ligature that is strangling her instead.

Let's look at this issue another way, starting with the cost of renting versus buying. When you rent, you have no mortgage with interest to pay, no expensive repairs or upkeep to pay for, no property taxes, no HOA fees, and none of the stress that homeowners have. Instead, you have the security of a roof over your head, a fixed monthly cost, and, best of all, you have the chance to move around and go places that you might never have considered when shackled with the responsibility of owning a home. Renting gives you freedom, and what better dream is there than freedom? We seem to have forgotten that's the *real* American dream.

DO ANY OF THESE QUESTIONS RESONATE WITH YOU?

1. Do you want to understand why you aren't achieving your goals all of the time?
2. Are you feeling stuck in some area of your life and you don't know how to get unstuck?
3. Do you keep seeing the same problem happening in your life, over and over again, and you can't seem to figure out why?
4. Do you know that you are a free spirit but just can't seem to live that way all of the time?

DO YOU RECOGNIZE ANY OF THESE ROADBLOCKS?

1. Why is it so hard, even impossible, to change?
2. It's impossible to get out of my current situation, so why even bother?
3. I can't be free to do what I want to do.
4. How do I get myself out of my burnout?
5. Why do I hate my job and my life so much?
6. How do I find the financial security that I know I deserve?

7. I don't know what happened to me. I used to be so happy.
8. I don't know what to do to make the changes.

When you are stuck in your life, your relationship, or your career, it's hard. When you feel helpless, you can hurt yourself and those around you when the accompanying anger, frustration and impatience surface. That's because when you are stuck, strong emotions are brewing within you. If you keep them buried and don't free these emotions, they have to go somewhere. And unfortunately, more often than not, they don't just disappear or rise slowly to the surface. They explode when you least expect them to at home, in the car, on a call with customer service, or on the job. You find yourself reacting in ways you're not used to. You lash out more often and are quick to the anger, frustration, and impatience that is lying just beneath the surface.

This emotional pain, when it continues for a long period of time, often leads to high levels of stress, anxiety, and eventually depression. When you get to the point of this type of depression, you're numb. You don't feel anything. If it goes on long enough, you're no longer able to lift your head above the fog. Before you know it, you're on medication. You want to make changes but you just don't seem to be able to get out of the funk. And that's when the helplessness and hopelessness settle in and take over.

Getting unstuck is about more than feeling good again. It could save your life.

I've watched what people go through in life with dismay,

frustration, and sadness. I chose to make change a big part of my life and have never stopped doing things that challenge me, scare the shit out of me, and make me a better person. Yes, I've been stuck. Yes, I've had times where I was struggling and I'm certainly not living a 'perfect' life now. But I've never sacrificed. And the rewards of living that life for me are that I'm a happy person most of the time and I'm free to do what I want to do. I'm independent. I make choices based on what it is that is best for me while taking into consideration those around me who will be affected. And I don't buy into the societal norms and expectations that most of us have had drilled into us all of our lives.

My ultimate goal is that, by changing our world one person at a time, we will build a larger mass movement and we will be able to live in a world that is not ruled by big business, the one percent, the corporate mindset, and employees who are afraid to quit because they are afraid of losing their benefits. The world will slowly become a place where people are independent of – not dependent upon – the government, corporations, and capitalism.

2
EXPECTATIONS: INTERNAL AND EXTERNAL

It's impossible to navigate your way through life without coming up against expectations. They are all around you, dictating so many of your choices. They are the external messages you get from society and your parents that you should do this and you shouldn't do that. You're told to choose one life-long career. You're told that you should get married, have children and retire when you're 65. Regardless of what your heart is saying, you feel obligated to follow these external expectations.

Then there are the internal messages. These are the things you tell yourself about what you should do and how you should live your life. You hear that voice inside your head reminding you to get back in line when you dare to imagine a life based on your own dreams and desires. While these internal expectations are shared by everyone, women deal with different messages than men.

WONDER WOMAN SYNDROME

As women, we tend to put all others before us. We try to do everything for everyone. We pride ourselves in our ability to multitask. We can be on the phone, sending emails, folding laundry, making dinner, and having an in-person conversation, all at once. Of course, that's not all. We will have every meeting organized, schedules coordinated, and conference calls set up. While it sounds impressive, and it is quite amazing to see women in action, this behavior causes great stress, exhaustion, anxiety, and is not sustainable without serious health, mental and emotional ramifications. It is called the Wonder Woman Syndrome.

I recently saw a television commercial where the wife was sick with the 'flu. Her husband was lying in bed sick as well, yet she was the one who was up, running around doing everything and taking care of everyone. She took the kids to school, brought the husband soup, did the laundry, all while running a high temperature and looking like death warmed over.

This is not about blaming the man, but looking at why it is that this woman thought she should be doing everything. She gets this from both internal and external expectations. It almost becomes an addiction for women to do it all. We feel needed, loved and important when we do. But until you are able to get out of the trees so you can see the entire forest, you don't see how unhealthy this behavior is. You aren't aware of the message it sends to your children, friends, coworkers, and the next generation's children. You're showing both sides, the boys and the girls, an example of unhealthy nurturing. You're also showing them that this is the way it should be. It's an expectation you've taken on that is now perpetuating itself.

What example do you want to set for your children? Do you want your daughter to grow up the same way, always putting the needs of others before herself? Do you want your son to become a man who expects that a woman is going to do everything for him? That he can sit on the couch and not give a hand to help?

These expectations are not something you can get rid of in one day, one week, or even one year. But once you understand what they are, you can finally do something about them – letting go of them layer by layer.

When you get on an airplane, you're instructed that in case of an emergency you are to put your own oxygen mask on first *before* helping someone else. As women, we've been putting everyone else's oxygen masks on in every situation and leaving our own until the very last, if we ever get it on at all. In the end, we are no good to anyone else if we aren't breathing.

We pride ourselves on our ability to be compassionate, loving and nurturing. Giving of ourselves to others is the way that we can be all of those things. And that feels good! Until it doesn't anymore, until we are drained and have given too much, too often, and too generously. Believe it or not, if you are willing to start taking time for yourself first, you will discover that it is possible to do it all and you'll feel much better to boot!

WHY DO THINGS JUST BECAUSE EVERYBODY ELSE DOES THEM?

Nancy was a recent client of mine. She'd been a nurse for more than 20 years. When Nancy first came to see me, she expressed how desperately she wanted a career change. Yet people around her kept saying, 'But you've been a nurse for so long. Why change now?' Meanwhile, her parents were saying, 'We put you through school for this. Do you know how much money we spent on your schooling? This is who you are. You are a nurse.' Yet she was miserable. She was stuck and bound by expectations that no longer worked for her. She had lost her passion for her job and her life – but she wouldn't leave. She kept listening to the expectations of others and her own internal expectations and beliefs until she started working with me and began to see how much it was costing her to stay where she was – both mentally and physically. After she came out on the other side of this struggle, she said to me, "I didn't realize how strong and how powerful the beliefs and expectations that I had were until you helped me see them, question them, and finally begin to change them."

Expectations affect your choices and therefore your ability to live a passionate life. But what would happen if you stopped doing things just because everybody else does them that way? How would your life be different? Where would you be right now? The answers to these questions will open up a whole new world for you if you're willing to go there.

FACING YOUR FEARS

What are some of your worst fears? What are the ones that keep you up at night and make it difficult for you to make a change? Do you ever dream of quitting your job, selling your house, and/or starting a completely new life somewhere else? Doing something entirely different?

If you do have a dream like any of these, what's stopping you? Chances are it is fear – based on some of the expectations we've been talking about. You're afraid to sell your house because it's been drilled into you that a house gives you financial security and is a sign of your success. You're afraid to quit your job because you've been told since you graduated from school that a job is something you hold on to for life. Jobs give you security and hopefully pay you a pension when you're older. To quit a good paying job is crazy, right? And you definitely shouldn't quit your current job until you find another. Just make sure the new job is in the same industry or field as the one you left. You certainly won't want to change careers mid-life because then you'd have to go back to school and compete with a younger crowd when you graduate.

Does any of this sound familiar? What are these objections really masking? It could be that once you start to look at your fear of selling your house, you realize that you have some seemingly crazy fear that you'll end up homeless one day. While you know deep down inside that you're not going to end up homeless if you don't own a house, where does that fear come from? Why is it there? If you turn it around and face it, just like facing the monster, you'll realize how silly that fear is.

THE COST OF LOSING YOUR FREEDOM

What if you are considering leaving a full-time job because you aren't happy there anymore? Many people who have worked all their lives as employees are afraid to take on a new job or career if it means they won't be employed with all of the benefits that come with employment. They think that's their security. And yet, as we've learned over the last 20 to 30 years, the shifting economy means that security is gone. There is no security in being an employee like there used to be years ago when pensions were the norm. But we still somehow have the belief that being an employee is going to keep us safe. In fact, I've found when working with clients who hate their jobs and want to move on to something more rewarding, the benefits package is the major talking point they use when they justify why they've stayed in a job or career so long, even when it's clear they are not happy there and haven't been for a while.

People believe the security of employee benefits is more important than freedom. We seem to ignore the cost – emotional, physical, psychological – of losing our freedom and our independence.

I want to encourage you to step away from your fear and the expectations society has placed on you, and that you have placed on yourself, and commit to finding your passion. Get your freedom and your independence back. That's how you discover and fulfill your passion.

3

CAREER BURNOUT

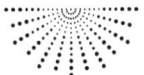

Career burnout is the number one issue I deal with in my program. I work with women who are tired of their careers and are frustrated, overwhelmed, and exhausted. They no longer have a passion for it. They may never have had a passion for it. Maybe at one time they thought they did, but now they're waking up and realizing it's just not what they want to do anymore. They feel it is time to finally have the freedom to do what they want to do.

The women I work with also want to find passion in life again. Many of the women I coach want their work schedule to be more flexible. They don't want to be tied to a desk in a nine-to-five job. I see a lot of people from the healthcare industry, from upper management positions, and from human resources. They're burned out and exhausted, but they still want to help people. What they don't want is to keep doing things in the same way they have been doing for years. They are ready to change.

SIGNS OF BURNOUT

Here are seven signs that indicate you may be suffering from burnout. How many of these do you identify with?

1. Dread: You dread getting up in the morning and going to work.
2. Emotional outbursts: You're easily irritated and frustrated with others.
3. Overwhelmed: You feel overwhelmed and anxious on a daily basis.
4. Over-medicating/overeating: You rely on medicines, alcohol and/or comfort foods to get through the day and night.
5. Hopelessness: You've given up and stopped hoping things can change.
6. Falling behind: You can't keep up with everything you used to be able to do.
7. Chronic illness: You have developed an autoimmune disorder or other chronic stress-related illness. You often catch colds and feel sick.

If you can relate to *any* of these, you're depleting yourself energetically and it's time to restore your body's balance before your burnout begins to destroy your relationships, your career, and your health.

Throughout this book, I'll share stories with you on how my unique eight-week program *Unleash Your Free Spirit: Change Your Life* has helped hundreds of women who, like you, were suffering from career burnout, find passion and fulfillment in their new lives.

USE WHAT YOU ALREADY KNOW TO CHANGE CAREERS

The answer to your career burnout may be hiding in plain sight, right smack in front of you. Many of the women I work with end up using what they already know to transition to a new career path. Some of them incorporate what they know into an online business, something more flexible that they can do from home. They might already have doctorate degrees, or they're a counsellor, or maybe they're in a corporate HR position, but they're ready to move on. They want to move into a coaching or other online business that allows them more flexibility and freedom. Starting a business that's more financially lucrative gives them a chance to be less tied down by obligations. What twist on your current career might be a better choice for you? Start to think outside of the box and you'll be surprised what you discover.

IT'S NEVER TOO LATE TO START OVER

It doesn't matter if you're 35, 45 or 55; it's never too late to start a new career, a new hobby, or a new life. Warren Buffet didn't start trading until after he was in his 50s. Colonel Sanders used his social security check to launch Kentucky Fried Chicken. They didn't let anything stand between them and their dreams. And they certainly didn't let a number like age get in their way. You shouldn't either.

4
LIMITING BELIEFS

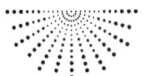

*L*imiting beliefs are the things we tell ourselves – and that society tells us – about how we should be living our lives. Limiting beliefs determine why we do what we do, what we are willing to stand for, and why we aren't able to make changes in our lives. They are the beliefs that we 'should' do this or we 'shouldn't' do that, regardless of what it is we want to do or know we can do.

Limiting beliefs steal our passion and sabotage our lives – and yet we listen to them. The more we listen, the harder it is to make the changes that we dream of making.

In our society, we tend to avoid looking at our limiting beliefs. We don't want to face them. Our tendency is to push them under the carpet. Like an ostrich, we put our heads in the sand and ignore them. We don't want to see them because it's easier to stay in denial than to look at the things that make us uncomfortable.

CHANGE YOUR BELIEFS AND YOU CHANGE YOUR DESTINY

If you heal your limiting beliefs, you can heal everything else, including the fears and emotions they generate, and change your destiny. You can change what you create.

What if you use limiting beliefs as a challenge for change; as impetus or motivation to change your life? To help you get started, I will give you some examples of specific limiting beliefs and how to change them. Once you understand their connection to how people become stuck, and consequently how they lose their passion, you will see how important it is to change these beliefs. This is how the beliefs then become motivators for change.

In the light of day, these limiting beliefs can even become something you can laugh at once you recognize, 'Oh yeah, there it is. That's when I sabotaged myself.'

When you begin to look at these societal and cultural expectations and then at all of our limiting beliefs, it can be overwhelming. You have to break it down step by step and the first step is to accept them. All you have to do is say, 'Yes, I have these beliefs and I have allowed them to guide my life.' Then you turn around, face the monster, and realize there is no monster after all.

By doing this, they no longer overwhelm you. Instead they become a part of your process that pushes you along toward the light at the end of the tunnel. Because there *is* a light at the end of this tunnel and I'm going to tell you how to get there.

After helping thousands of people change their lives, I've

found the seven most common limiting beliefs. They are so prevalent and may be so much a part of your psyche that you aren't even aware they are there, and yet they can make you surrender before you even get close to achieving your dreams. So let's reveal them and then remove them before they destroy your dreams.

1. I'M A VICTIM

We all have a bit of the victim mentality. In the extreme, victims embody this belief throughout their entire being. They're hard to be around and they unknowingly chase people away. You may know the type. They blame you for stuff that happens to them. They can't get anything done or be successful because they can't keep a job or a place to live. They can't be in relationships. Everything is defined because of something that happened *to* them that isn't their fault. A victim is the one that says, 'You'll never know what I'm going through. You'll never know how tough it is for me. So don't try to make it better for me.' They *want* to stay in it. Whereas someone who is choosing not to be a victim, but instead a creator of their life, looks at the things that have happened not as something that defines them, but rather as experiences to learn from and grow from. Their attitude is more glass half full than half empty. They would say, 'Yes, that happened to me and it sucked. It was terrible. But it's not something that I want to blame anybody – myself or anyone else for.'

The key to combatting a victim mentality is to get to the place where you decide how you're going to define things that have happened to you. You'll find it's much more empowering when you do.

Be positive. Notice when you start to sound like a victim and *choose* to change your behavior. Use this mantra: *I am the creator of my life and my experiences and I embrace them all.*

2. I'M NOT WORTHY

This is one of the classic limiting beliefs. It boils down to thinking you're not good enough. And if you're not good enough then you can't possibly make the changes in your life that you want to make. Many of us carry this belief from childhood. We grow up with it and we see it in our parents, our grandparents, and in our society's norms.

There are definite gender differences with this belief. For women, I call it being a sacrificial lamb. It says, 'I must put everyone else before me. I'm being selfish to want what I want. I'm selfish to do what I want to do.' To begin letting go of this false belief, start turning it on its head by being a little selfish. For example, when you come home and have a million and one things to do, consider what items on your to-do list can be done by another family member and ask them to help you out. If you have trouble with this, start with just one thing, let go of it and see how it feels.

For men, this limiting belief is best described as 'it's all on me'. In our society, men are defined by what they do and not who they are, and so they carry a huge responsibility. They learn this as young boys. They grow up to be men who in many ways feel that they are defined by their career choice.

This choice is connected to how they feel they perform as a father, a husband, and a provider. Of course, not all men feel this way. But it's important for women to understand that a vast majority of men feel it is their responsibility to take care of everything and everyone. Whether it's true or not, they feel the burden of the family's financial wellbeing, that it is up to them to put food on the table and keep a roof over the family's head. It's all on them. Therefore for men, it limits their ability to dream and think outside the box in terms of life changes.

Whether you're a woman or a man, when you start to see and understand this limiting belief from both sides, you can see how conflicts and misunderstandings happen. You will see how important it is to have compassion for each other, so you can work together to make a more mutually beneficial relationship and support each other as you begin to make significant life changes.

3. SELF-DOUBT

This is that voice within that says, 'I don't believe I can do it. I can't make this change. It's not going to happen.' It's a subtle yet powerful voice that often shows up unexpectedly. If you look at your dream right now, where are you limiting it based on your doubts?

Let's take my dream, which is to reach hundreds of thousands, even millions of people, with my business, The Free Spirit Project. I can feel the energy of the dream. I can see what the project looks like when I have reached all of those people. But still, sometimes I think I'm crazy to dream so big. I can hear a voice in my head telling me it's never going to happen and I'll never reach that many people. That is the voice of self-doubt showing up. Usually it's a voice that's been there so long you don't realize it's there, until someone else catches you saying it out loud. When it shows up for me in relation to my dream to reach millions of people, I say to myself, 'Yes, it's possible that it won't happen, but I'm going to hold on to the belief that it will happen and I'm going to keep working on my dream.' It's as simple as that. I don't let it stop me from moving forward.

4. I'M NOT DESERVING

> "No one can make you feel inferior without your consent."
>
> — ELEANOR ROOSEVELT

I'd like to note that some of the beliefs I'm describing in this chapter are similar and can even overlap. The limiting belief 'I'm not deserving' is very similar to the first belief 'I'm not worthy'. It's also similar to 'self-doubt'. I've chosen to split up these beliefs for the purposes of my program because there are nuances of each that I think are important to look at and identify.

The 'I'm not deserving' belief is the voice that says, 'I don't deserve to have everything I want or dream of or desire.' It's a dream crusher. Recognize when it shows up and how it starts to crush your dream. Acknowledge it. Acknowledging it is half the battle and often simply staring right at this limiting belief will cause it to lose its power.

The first time I became aware of this limiting belief was when I was in my twenties. I had realized corporate America wasn't for me and I had to leave. I decided to take off and start traveling around the world. It was scary. I left my safe, secure world to go out there alone and challenge myself. The limiting belief that I didn't deserve this kept popping up. People were saying to me, 'You're so lucky to be able to do that,' or 'Oh, God, I could never do that. I wouldn't be able to take off and leave everything.' I would hear that and start thinking to myself, 'I don't deserve this either. I don't deserve to have what I want, what I dream.'

Those people were mirroring my limiting belief to me. But I didn't let it stop me. I recognized it for what it was: the monster in the closet. As soon as I turned around and faced it, it no longer held any power over me.

Once you are able to acknowledge that you are afraid, that maybe you feel you aren't worthy of your dreams, that you might not be able to achieve them, you have faced the monster. You can finally turn the monster into the teddy bear that it really is and no longer let it stop you.

5. SCARCITY

Scarcity is a powerful limiting belief. It is part of our daily lives. We believe we have a limited amount of just about everything on this planet. I remember back in the '70s (when I was just a wee baby, I'm sure), there was all this talk about how we were going to run out of fuel and all of these key resources within 10 years. Yet here we are 40 years later and that didn't happen. In so many ways, we let fear of scarcity limit us. We believe we don't have enough resources, enough time, and certainly not enough money. The fear of not having enough money, or of running out of money, is one of the main reasons people don't follow their dreams. The amazing thing is, when you let go of the limiting belief of scarcity, it's incredible how much you can actually achieve. Opportunities show up, people show up, and money shows up.

When I was going through my MBA program, I remember reading a book about a man who decided to see how he could function without any money. He took a bus to a city that was at least a day trip away so he couldn't get back home easily. He had no money with him except the money he needed to buy the one-way bus ticket. His whole goal was to see how he could function and survive without any money in a completely strange city where he didn't know anyone. What it taught him was how resourceful he could be when that happens.

He ended up working for his meal at a restaurant. Then he cleaned tables to earn a place to sleep. At each step of his journey, he was open and willing to step out of his comfort zone and he was able to manifest food, a place to sleep, and money for the trip back home. He met some amazing people on the way.

When I was traveling in Australia, I decided to try his experiment for myself to see what would happen. I got off the ferry in Tasmania and went into a youth hostel. I told the woman at registration that I didn't have any money and I asked if there was some way I could work for room and board. At first, she looked at me like I was nuts. (I did actually have money but that was not the purpose of this.) I said it again. 'I don't have any money, I need to find a place to work for room and board.' She still looked at me like I was nuts and told me I could give her my passport to hold until I could get to the bank the next day. So, I said it a third time and this time she gave me a suggestion. She told me about a woman who was about 30 or 40 miles out in the middle of nowhere who was setting up a wildlife reserve and needed help. The directions to get to the place were to drive 30 miles, turn left onto the only crossroad, and after about 3 or 4 miles I would see goats grazing at the side of the road. That would be my destination. I ended up staying there for three weeks, learning all about the indigenous plants and animals of Tasmania. She gave me room and board and I worked pulling weeds and doing odd jobs she needed done. It was a chance to take money out of the picture and have a life-changing experience because I chose not to be limited by fears.

For me and the fellow in my MBA book, the challenge and lesson learned was how limited we are when we think of things in such finite ways as there 'isn't enough' and how much we limit our options when we use money as our only way to barter.

Change your belief instead to abundance and, as Deepak Chopra says, "unlimited possibilities" and you will experience magic and miracles everywhere you go.

6. SELF-SABOTAGE

We've all experienced this limiting belief. It goes like this: 'I don't know how to do it so I won't. It's going to take forever to learn this new thing I want to do so I might as well not try.' We've all been there. It's like the children's story called *The Little Engine That Could*. I loved that story from my childhood. It was about getting a long train up over a high mountain. Large engines were asked to pull the train but they had the sabotaging belief that they couldn't do it. The belief was so strong for them that even if they tried they couldn't do it. Meanwhile the little engine had the opposite voice going over and over in its head: "I think I can. I think I can." And finally, he got the train up over the hill.

Self-sabotage is one of the main reasons people don't switch careers. They tell themselves it's too late to change careers. Or they put feelers out there for a new type of career and take the first perceived negative thing that happens as a reason to give up. Maybe they hear nobody is hiring anyone over 40, so they give up then and there, thinking they'll never get hired. People sabotage their chances before they even try. When you hear the voice that says, 'It's too hard... it's taking too long... I don't think I can do it,' stop. Listen. Then flip it around and say, 'Do I want to keep doing that? Do I want to keep sabotaging myself every time I start something? Or do I want to acknowledge that's what I'm doing here and just move through it?' It's time to say "I think I can! I think I can!"

7. I'M A FAILURE

This limiting belief is double-barreled: I'm a failure – and I need to be perfect. Because I'm not perfect, I am a failure.

These may seem different but they're two sides of the same coin. We don't allow for mistakes in this society. It's damaging to fail, especially these days where everything is much more in the public eye.

Sometimes the fear of failure is so great it stops people from ever pursuing their dreams. They believe they have to be perfect and have it all figured out before they even begin. But the only way to do something new is to start somewhere and learn it. So, if you're finding yourself stopping because you're not good enough at it yet, or you're not perfect, this is the belief that's stopping you from doing it.

Mistakes and failures are just opportunities to learn and grow. What's so bad about that? If everyone let this limiting belief stop them from getting started, we wouldn't have airplanes, electricity, cars, and every other invention known to man.

Thomas Edison said, "I have not failed. I have just found 10,000 ways that won't work."

Michael Jordan said, "I've missed more than 9,000 shots in my career. I've lost almost 300 games. 26 times I've been trusted to take the game-winning shot and I missed. I've failed over and over and over again in my life. That is why I succeed."

Don't give up before you start – let your invention/creation be shared with the world!

LET GO OF THE SEVEN KILLER LIMITING BELIEFS

Change your beliefs and you change your destiny. You don't have to be stuck with any of these beliefs. I know. I've been working on them since I started this process for myself. As I work through layers and layers of them, I get more joyful. My world is more peaceful. And I am happy to say that it gets easier.

MANTRA CARD

I have a Free Spirit mantra card, which includes the seven limiting beliefs and the opposite self-affirming belief for each, available for download on my website. You can laminate it and keep it with you at all times. Just go to the Additional Resources page at the end of this book and find the link.

SECTION 2: BABY STEPS TO BIG DREAMS

5

MY STORY

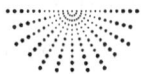

My first limiting belief has its roots in an incident when I was only four years old. I've never forgotten because I was so embarrassed and humiliated. I was with my family and we were standing in line waiting to go to a restaurant at the University of Michigan. We were in the hall of the Michigan League waiting for the doors to open. I had to go to the bathroom and my mom let me go into the bathroom by myself. I felt so big and grown up. I had three older siblings, so for me to be able to do what I'd watched all my older siblings do was a big deal for me. I went into the bathroom on my own and I came out feeling so proud of myself.

Then this woman called me over to her as I was walking back down the hall to where my family was in line. As I was walking, I passed by a whole bunch of people and I was wondering what she wanted to say to me. She reached down and pulled my skirt out of my tights. I had walked proudly past all these people with my skirt tucked into my tights. I was so humiliated, ashamed, and embarrassed.

I've never forgotten that experience. And yet why did I feel those feelings at that age? Where did they come from? Somebody else might walk out of that door, have that happen, say, 'Whatever,' and have no trauma around it at all. But for me, at the age of four, I took up my first limiting belief: 'I'm a failure. I'm not perfect.' Along with that belief came feelings of humiliation and embarrassment. What I took away from that was that I would not try to do anything that put me out there. Heck, I wasn't even capable of going on my own to the washroom without looking like a fool!

But if I had stopped there and never challenged this limiting belief, I wouldn't have done many of the things I have done in my life. If I just let the fear of being embarrassed and humiliated take over, I would have never performed as a singer on stage and I most certainly would never have started doing this work. Instead, I used this limiting belief as a challenge to change. And what I have discovered as I keep putting myself out there is that the limiting belief no longer has its hold on me like it did. I guess you could say I'm fine looking foolish now.

BACK TO THE BEGINNING

I grew up in the Midwest. I thought I would do everything the way my parents had done it. I even became a Certified Public Accountant (CPA) because my dad was a CPA and I seemed to have a knack for numbers. I was engaged to be married. I had a high school sweetheart and we went all the way through college together. We were going to move to Chicago and live the yuppie life there. I was doing everything that I thought I was supposed to do. But one day I woke up and realized I didn't even know myself. I found myself wondering if this was what life was about. I ended up breaking off the engagement. It was the first major decision I made that would change the course of my life.

I ended up moving to Chicago by myself, became a CPA, got my MBA, and had a blast living life in the big city. After a while, I began to wonder once again if there wasn't more to life than this for me. One morning I sat straight up in bed and knew that it was time for me to leave. I decided I wanted to challenge myself by working my way around the world.

And that's when fears started coming. What were people going to think? I was terrified to tell people. I wasn't sure how my parents would react because my dad had put me through college. Would he be upset because I was 'throwing away' my career? What were my friends and my co-workers going to think? I also had huge fear about leaving my job, like I was going to end up starving and freezing on the streets. They were crazy fears but they came up.

What I discovered through that process was when you're making changes, if you're afraid and you ask everybody else for their opinion, they will mirror your fears right back to you. And those fears will keep you from doing things, if you let them.

I decided to take off to Australia and ended up working my way around the country for two years. That was the first time

I did something that really scared me. It wasn't easy. I challenged myself over and over again and I faced a lot of fears. I was looking for something – exactly what, I didn't know. And I wasn't going to discover what it was until quite a few years later.

A LITTLE HELP FROM A FRIEND

I continued to do a lot of traveling when I returned to the States. Then a couple of years later I started backpacking around the Middle East, into Africa, and over to India. I spent almost two years doing that. Before I left for that trip, I met a Los Angeles producer named Nick Venet. He'd produced the Beach Boys, Linda Ronstadt, and Sam Cooke, to name a few. I started studying songwriting under him for the two years I was back in the States. Then I took off again. I disappeared. At one point, Nick sent me a birthday card. I don't remember where I was in the world and I was surprised to get a card from him. He wrote something like, "You don't have to go running all around looking for love. You can come home, you'll find it right here." At the time I got his card, I didn't understand the significance of his message. It was much later when I realized that he had identified what I was looking for, only it wasn't just love that I was seeking. I was running and searching for freedom, for independence. But it was not something I could find by traveling. I didn't have to go anywhere to find it. It was all within.

That was the beginning for me of understanding what I

wanted to do with my life: to help people understand that it is all within.

But first I still had some truths to face about what it means to be a free spirit.

MY 'AHA' MOMENT

I continued to travel. At one point, I was roaming the islands of Fiji for two months and working on writing songs. I ended up on a very small island that took 10 minutes to walk around. The locals would bring food over to us on a boat and they'd cook in a little shack. There were only ten huts on the island. One night, I met a guy who was not afraid to say what he thought. He was the kind of person who knew how to push people's buttons. He had no qualms about expressing his feelings and doing whatever he wanted to do. I was much more reserved, quiet, and concerned with how I affected other people. One afternoon, we were all hanging around the picnic tables where we ate our meals and he looked at me and said, "Martha, you think you're a free spirit, but you're never going to be one."

It was probably one of the most painful things anyone has ever said to me. I had challenged myself and traveled around the world for years. I'd done things that not only scared me but would scare other people, too. I'd faced my fears. I believed all this made me a free spirit. Yet here was this guy who saw right through me. I wasn't a free spirit. I was trapped in this shell of my own making and was never going to be a free spirit being the way I was.

Though it was painful to be exposed for who I truly was, it didn't stop me from searching for the true meaning of being a free-spirited woman. It was thanks to this chance encounter with a free-spirited man that my journey to truly being a free-spirited woman began. Well, that encounter and another with a remarkable woman named Gingie Johnson.

6
BEING A FREE SPIRIT

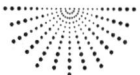

There is no single definition for what a free spirit is and what being one encompasses. If I attempt a definition myself, perhaps being a free spirit is simply finding the freedom within to do what you want to do with your life, whatever that is. I see it as being more independent, not co-dependent on other people, and moving through blocks and challenges at your own pace so you can get to where you want to be.

INSPIRED BY A FREE-SPIRITED WOMAN

Gingie Johnson is a legend in Australia in certain circles. She is the epitome of my definition of a free spirit. Originally from Kansas, she moved to Australia when she was 30. By the time I met her she had been there for 25 years. She owned a sailboat and was chartering boats and sailing, doing what she loved.

She was also an artist. She was living the life she wanted and created.

It wasn't always that way for Gingie. She had been working as an art professor for close to 20 years in Melbourne when she had a very bad and public breakup with her partner of 15 years. What did Gingie do? She left her old life behind, got on her boat, and started sailing up the east coast of Australia by herself to start a new life in the tropics.

Since then, tales of Gingie surviving all kinds of calamities spread across the sailing community of Australia. She went on to teach and mentor women, including me. She taught me not to be afraid to do what I want to do. She taught me what it meant to be a free-spirited woman.

TRAITS OF A FREE-SPIRITED WOMAN

These traits are excerpted from an article published in April 2017 by Mind, Body, Green.

1. **Confidence.** As a free spirit, you know that you are an amazing being (and so is everyone else) even though you may not feel that way all the time.
2. **Independence.** You make decisions that are best for you and don't let others hold you back or restrict you. Still, you come from a place of accountability and responsibility for your actions.
3. **Positivity.** You choose to look at the world in a positive way regardless of all the negativity you see around you. Your glass isn't half-empty or half-full.

Your glass is full and you are going to keep it that way!
4. **Courage.** As a free spirit, you don't shy away from change because you know that there is nothing more satisfying in life than being able to look back and say, 'I did it!'
5. **Determination.** You won't stop reaching for your dreams just because others have told you you'll never make it. You KNOW you can!
6. **Resilience.** You get back up when you've fallen. Even when the fall is a big one, you won't let it stop you from reaching for your dreams.
7. **Self-assurance.** You get that the world is a place of unlimited possibilities, even if you're not able to tap into all of those possibilities in this moment.

What happens when you describe yourself as possessing each of these traits? Try them out. Say, 'I am confident. I am independent,' and so on. How does it feel to call yourself confident, independent, positive, courageous, determined, resilient, and self-assured? Do you feel intimidated or uncomfortable?

The most important thing to remember is that you don't have to be perfect to be a free spirit. You don't have to fully embody these traits in every single moment to be a free spirit. All you have to do is set an intention to live your life to the best of your ability and strive to achieve the traits that are important to you.

It is up to you to make the changes in your life that bring you the joy and excitement that life has in store for you. Your path is yours and no one else's. No one can do it but you. And that is the most freeing possibility of all.

Whether it's sailing solo up the coast of Australia, starting a non-profit to rescue animals, or rekindling your passion for your current career, doing what you love is the path to freedom. That's the most important lesson I learned from Gingie in Australia and from the free-spirited man on the islands of Fiji. It has become my passion to help others feel what it is to be free and a free spirit. This is what my total motivation is for why I do what I do: why I teach and why I started The Free Spirit Project.

How about you? What's your motivation? Why do you do what you do?

SECTION 3: CHANGE YOUR LIFE, CREATE, AND COMMIT

7
BE THE CREATOR OF YOUR OWN LIFE

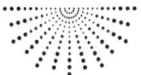

The key to my *Unleash Your Free Spirit: Change Your Life* program is to get you to think outside of the box. One of my clients, Cathy, was in her 50s and had raised her two daughters on her own. They were now grown and out on their own, and Cathy was going through the 'empty nest' feeling of loss. She came to me because she was stressed and overwhelmed. She had a house that she was keeping for her girls, but she worked four jobs to keep it. She was continually over-stressing her body and her emotions were working overtime. She was burnt out and ready to change. Of all the things that we talked about, I asked her what was the most stressful thing right now. It was the house. But when she considered selling it in order to get herself into the position where she didn't have to work so hard to pay for a home, she had a lot of fears come up. In our culture, we don't encourage somebody to sell a house unless they are planning on buying another one right away. To be without a house can be very scary for many people because they think they'll lose their safety and security. That is just what Cathy witnessed when she decided to sell her home. Many of her friends and acquaintances said things to her like, 'Don't sell the house. You've got to keep it. It's an investment.'

NOTHING CHANGES IF NOTHING CHANGES

After working with me, Cathy came to understand the cost of hanging on to this expectation of home ownership – to her life and her physical and financial health. When she finally sold the house, her life changed unbelievably. She was able to do things that she had wanted to do all her life. She'd never been to Europe, so she took a trip there on her own. She lived in the mountains of Colorado for a couple of ski seasons. She's much more open to change now. And the best part is that she sleeps through the night!

Learning how to be a free spirit and understanding the power it gives you to make choices that are right for you is life changing. You find passion again. You find excitement. You don't wake up with anxiety. You wake up ready to get out of bed and do whatever it is you want to do. If you want to make major life changes, you're excited about it now. You're ready to do it.

Are you ready to get started? Are you ready to change your life and unleash your free spirit? Let's go!

SETTING INTENTIONS

The first thing you need to do is set your intention for what you want to achieve and accomplish. There are all kinds of intentions. You can set a major life intention, you can set an intention for the day, for a yoga class, even one for this program. It's so important to set your intention at the very beginning so that you state what you want to create. This will help to keep you focused on your goals and 'hold the space' or make room for whatever it is you want to create.

INTRODUCTION TO THE FREE SPIRIT PROJECT

Think about elite athletes. They don't get to the Olympics by doing everything all by themselves. Athletes, musicians, even corporate executives, all have coaches to help them.

Coaching will provide a way for you to bounce ideas and thoughts off others, to get feedback so you know where you're stuck, and to isolate the areas you want and need to improve in your life.

The Free Spirit Project is about helping people change their lives. We will work on unleashing your free spirit through a combination of online learning materials and coaching (in groups and one-on-one). Both are beneficial in helping people move through their stuff. The group coaching helps you learn vicariously through others. It's amazing what you may miss in yourself until you actually see it in someone else. After spending years working with people only in a one-on-one coaching environment, I found the group coaching method so much more valuable for exactly this reason. My clients have so many more 'aha' moments when they listen to someone else share their experiences than when they work alone on their stuff. I've also found it best to have clients come through my eight-week program first so that they can jump-start their progress and experience the group and one-on-one coaching firsthand. Then they can decide what it is they need to move forward after that.

THE IMPORTANCE OF COACHING

For some reason here in the United States, we don't seem to put a lot of emphasis on self-development, at least monetarily. We'll pay for our academic education. We'll pay for our health care. But for whatever reason, when it comes to our own self-development, personal improvement, and helping ourselves live our dream lives, we think we shouldn't put money into it. There seems to be this strange thinking that it's something we should be able to do on our own, or by reading books and going to inspirational talks. And that's how we end up miserable and exhausted instead.

When you look at successful people, they will tell you that they have coaches. Take Oprah Winfrey, for example. She freely admits that she has coaches. She has people that help her all the time. And they're not just friends offering an ear. Oprah actually seeks out coaches to help her in many areas of her life. She looks at where she knows she has some weaknesses and where she's stuck and can't move forward, and she will pay to get help.

It's important to invest in your self-development because you will take it more seriously. The more you are willing to invest, the more serious you will be about doing it.

A coach should be somebody you don't know personally. You don't want your partner or a friend because they're too close to you and they tend to have their own biases when it comes to what is 'good' for you. It's best to find someone who doesn't know you so they can be completely unbiased and help you see things that someone close to you is not able to help you see.

LIFE GETS IN THE WAY

The next thing to look at when trying to figure out why you aren't making change happen, is what I call the 'life gets in the way' factor. You want to acknowledge this up front because often the reason you don't move towards what you want is that you don't have enough time in the day to add the additional tasks you need to do in order to make this happen.

There are only so many hours in a day and days in a week. If your schedule is already booked to overflowing then you won't be able to make change happen until you free up some time. You can't start reaching for a new dream if you aren't giving yourself the time and the space to create it. You have to look at all of your commitments: work, family, social, hobbies, sports activities, and personal downtime. What are your commitments and how do you use your day? You're going to need to let go of something that's on your schedule now in order to add something new.

Write everything down, including your work hours, commitments, how much time you spend cooking, driving the kids around, and so on. Write down everything in three columns. In column one list things that are necessary and that you can't let go of right now. Column two is for things that are questionable; you'd rather not let go of them but they're not necessary. The third column is for the things you *can* let go of. Then take that third column, set your intention to let these activities go, and burn them so that you can bring in the new. Have a ceremony. This step is critical because if you aren't willing to make the room, you are not going to make the changes that you need to make to accomplish your dreams.

In addition to the normal daily/weekly/monthly activities on your calendar, you will find that distractions show up right when you are about to make that important phone call or send out that potentially life-changing email. If you are willing to look at your patterns and see what it is that you either allow or invite to get in the way, you will be able to recognize them when they show up and take steps to remove these distractions before they stop you in your tracks again. For instance, all of a sudden you decide you need to work 50 hours a week. Or you have family projects and other items on your 'to do' list that you decide have to get done and they absolutely MUST be done right now. These are the things that get in the way. The things that stop us from making the changes we need to make in order to achieve our dreams. They are how we sabotage ourselves.

For example, whenever I am ready to start something, all of a sudden I decide I need to organize my sock drawer, or I need to clean the bathroom, or go through my basement and find things that I can donate to Goodwill. While the tasks of organizing, cleaning and donating are all 'noble' and/or healthy things to do, I don't need to do them *right now.* They are tasks that I'm using to avoid making changes that my ego is afraid to make.

Come up with a list of things that you know you have used in the past to distract yourself, whether they're family distractions or extra projects at work. Acknowledge them and write them down. You have to be willing to set the intention, acknowledge that things get in the way, and then clear out your space so that you have time and energy for your new and exciting life.

Now you're ready to make the changes.

8
IN THE FLOW

Have you ever been in the 'flow'? Do you remember when you felt great doing something that you loved? That feeling when time just seemed to fade away because you were so into what you were doing.

Athletes describe being in the flow when they are competing. Runners will begin to prep themselves well ahead of a race by visualizing the race and how it will go for them. When they step up to the starting line, their mind and body are focused on one thing and one thing only: the race. As the gun goes off and they begin to run, everything else disappears. They don't hear the crowd. They are running and nothing else matters. Everything happens easily and rhythmically. Time doesn't seem to exist. They may even describe a feeling of euphoria that comes over them as they are running. They are in the flow.

When you are in the flow, you feel unstoppable. Everything is going your way. Everything you ask for comes to you.

Things start showing up. You start meeting the right people. You feel excitement and joy. Your life is thrilling. You're on top of the world.

The other aspect of being in the flow that is often overlooked is that you're willing to face your fears and do things that have been hard for you in the past. Flow doesn't mean that there are no obstacles that show up in your life; those obstacles simply become easier to handle. When you're totally in the flow, you know that everything's going to work out. It doesn't even matter what other people tell you. In fact, you will hear highly successful people talk about all the naysayers in life who told them whatever it was they were doing would never work. And they will tell you that they didn't listen to those naysayers and they just kept living their dream.

For me, I know when I'm in the flow because I get a warm fuzzy feeling in my heart. It is a feeling of wellbeing and contentment. For you, it might be a feeling in your stomach or in your head, or a general feeling all over your body. Corporate America calls it being in the zone. Everything progresses easily and just works. When you're in the flow, you're happy. You don't let things bring you down.

Both happiness and flow are choices that you make. You have to choose happiness and you have to choose to be in the flow. You don't just sit around and do nothing and end up in the flow. You have to choose it all the time.

In order to experience your life in the flow, it's helpful to go into your past and look at when you've actually felt like you were in the flow, so that you can identify what that felt like for you.

Then as you go through my program, we'll take a look at when you've been out of the flow. We want to start identifying this so that you can tap back into the positive feelings and know what puts you in the flow (and what takes you out). By knowing what the feelings are, we can recreate your experiences of being in the flow as you move forward and begin to live your dream life.

IN THE FLOW – EXERCISE 1

Go back through your life and identify the first time you remember being in the flow. When you were a child, what do you remember doing where you didn't notice time passing because you were so in the moment or in the zone? Then do this again, picking other experiences from your life. The goal is to try to come up with the top ten flow experiences of your life.

For example, I can remember several times I was in the flow as a kid, mostly involving times I was acting or singing on stage. As I got older, I was in the flow when I travelled. Indeed, I was in the flow for a long time in Australia. I'd set the intention when I left the States that I was going to go and challenge myself. I wanted to prove that I could do things on my own and do things that I didn't think I could do. While I was challenged and I was scared many times, I was also in the flow. Even as I felt fear, things always worked out, people showed up when I needed them, I was in the right place at the right time over and over again, and everything came together perfectly in the end. I was in the flow because of the fact that I was willing to continue to face my fears and move through them.

How many times have you experienced the flow? Write them down. You are going to use them in the next exercise.

IN THE FLOW – EXERCISE 2

Pick at least three of your flow moments and do a visualization exercise. Visualize being in the experience again and feel it in your body. Remember what it felt like. Did you feel calm and focused? Did you notice everything sort of fade away around you?

Then write it down. Don't judge or censor yourself. Write down everything you remember. What were you thinking? How did it feel? Where were you? How long did it last? Look for patterns or common denominators in your flow experiences. Look for the common feelings you had and what you were doing when you were in the flow. For me, a pattern among my flow experiences was that I was always pushing through some fear or doing something that was challenging, like traveling alone or performing on stage. While another common denominator I had was the feeling that everything was right with the world, I was on a natural 'high'.

Even have a bit of fun with this exercise. Try picking a theme song based on your experiences in life and play it. Find a song that works for you and use it to call up the feelings of being in the flow. I have several songs that work for me, but two of my favorites are Steve Winwood's "Higher Love" and "Jump" by Van Halen.

THE KINKS - WHEN YOU ARE NOT IN THE FLOW

At the opposite end from flow are the kinks, which are the blocks to flow or the obstacles that hold you back and keep you from achieving your dreams. These are the things that aren't working. These kinks in the line are there to show you when you aren't in the flow and that you should start to consider making some adjustments because it just might get more painful if you keep doing what you are doing.

If we look at flow like a river, then the kinks are the obstacles that get in the way or the obstacles that we create ourselves. For instance, sometimes we hang onto the big boulder in the middle of the river while water threatens to drown us and it's getting painful. Yet all we have to do is let go of the boulder, turn around onto our backs, and float down the river.

Life is much easier when you go with the flow rather than fight it.

A DIFFERENT KIND OF BUCKET LIST EXERCISE

Just like you did with the flow exercise, look back through your life and find the times when you were struggling. Create a different kind of bucket list here by identifying what didn't work and still isn't working now.

Ask yourself, 'How many times has happened in my life? What's the impact on me now? Are these kinks the reason you are where I am now?'

Look at what's NOT working and create your bucket list,

breaking it down into the following areas:

- work
- personal (physical health, emotional, spiritual)
- social (friends, past relationships, old roommates)
- family, and
- money (financial, investments).

Don't think about it too much, just start writing and get it out as it comes to you. Delve into your past. Be willing to face issues that you may not have resolved yet. Instead of creating a bucket list of what you want to do, this is the list of things that you *don't* want to be doing but you find you're still doing. Where did you ignore something for too long and it got painful?

You don't want to get wrapped up into the story around every issue. You want to step outside of yourself and be very objective about it (as best as you can anyway). It's time to move out of denial and to acknowledge that these are the reasons you are stuck right now. You're not going to move forward if you don't acknowledge the things that are keeping you stuck.

Disclaimer: This exercise is meant to help you discover and uncover moments in your life that haven't gone well for you. However, if it causes too much pain and discomfort to bring these things up, don't go there. Seek professional help.

After you've created your list, begin to look for patterns or common themes on your list. For me, I discovered I don't work well in corporate America. The corporate environment doesn't suit me. Yet I kept taking corporate jobs because they were easy for me to get and they paid well. Every time I started working in that environment I would start to hate everything about it – the fluorescent lights, the sterile office building, the nine to five routine – and I started to seriously dislike myself, the job, and everyone that worked there. It was a toxic environment for me. So, the sooner I stopped looking for jobs and opportunities in corporate America, the sooner I got myself back in the flow. And it worked. I don't even consider corporate jobs anymore because I know how much they drain the energy from me.

Remember, it's not about beating yourself up. It's about taking an objective look at what's been holding you back. If you don't acknowledge these things, you will stay in denial and keep lying to yourself. In fact, denial actually stands for:

D = **D**on't
E = **E**ven
N = k**N**ow
I = **I**
A = **A**m
L = **L**ying (to myself)

Get out of denial, identify the kinks and admit the truth. Look at all the things you are doing that keep you from fulfilling your dreams so you can start letting them go.

Up to now, you've taken a good, hard look at your life. You acknowledged the things that work and the things that don't work. You admitted the ways you've sabotaged yourself. Well done. Now we're going to step away from the observer perspective and go within to discover your passion. Now it's time to dream.

9
DREAM DISCOVERY

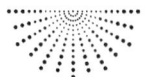

*I*t's time to dream! This is where the real fun begins. Creating your dream is the chance to think way outside the box. What do you want to do? What do you want your life to look like? Paint a picture in your mind. Imagine your whole life, everything you want to create in all areas: your dream job, your dream partnership, your dream lifestyle, everything. What do you want to create?

To begin with, believe that anything is possible. There are no limitations. Go as big as you can. This is about the big picture. Identify the dream life you know you deserve, that is your birthright, the one you have always known you should have.

When you visualize your dream, take money out of the equation. Money is often the biggest limitation and it doesn't need to be. If you limit yourself by saying, 'I can't do that because I don't have the money,' you are selling yourself short. You have just taken yourself out of the dream game before you even started. There are many ways to manifest your dreams and using money is only one of those ways. I know of three people who needed a car and had someone give them a car. If they had set the limitation that they needed to buy a car, they would have not been open to the other possibilities and might have missed out on a perfect opportunity.

Look at your life with the fresh eyes of a child. Go back to that feeling of awe and wonder that you had when you were young. The purpose of visualizing your dream is so that you can pull up this vision, and the feelings that you had during the visualization, at any time. This is so important for longevity. When you are six months, two years or five years into your dream and you have hit a significant roadblock, you'll be less likely to give up if you can remember what it is you are doing this for.

DREAM DISCOVERY MEDITATION

Meditation is a powerful tool for creating and manifesting. It is used to reduce stress and anxiety, heal physical ailments, and for just about anything you can think of that will move you towards a positive, peaceful, joyful life. Meditation has been used for eons to help masters, great visionaries, and even lesser known or recognized people create their worlds. There are as many meditation techniques as there are people teaching them and sharing them.

The dictionary definition of meditate is 'to think deeply or focus one's mind for a period of time, in silence or with the aid of chanting, for religious or spiritual purposes or as a method of relaxation'.

It's that simple! 'To think deeply or focus one's mind for a period of time...' Meditating doesn't mean you have to sit for hours. Nor does it mean you have to clear your mind completely. In fact, you don't even have to sit. You don't even have to be completely silent. You can choose to meditate on any topic you want. You can do meditative walks, runs, swims. You can be meditating in the midst of chaos if you are willing to do it.

Meditating doesn't have to be this major process of getting yourself in a pretzel position, clearing your mind completely, and keeping it clear for hours on end. You just have to decide what it is you want to get out of your meditation and trust that there is a benefit in doing it. This isn't rocket science. It's simply common sense. Slow down for a minute, take a few deep breaths, and get in touch with yourself again. You'll like what you discover.

The meditation that I'm going to show you is simple and requires so little effort that all you have to do is just listen to the audio and you'll be surprised by how easy and fun it is. It's a micro training session on the process of meditation. If you go to the Additional Resources section of this book, you will find the link to the audio session where I will guide you through meditation. I will also give you ideas about how to approach this manifestation if you have more than one dream or you want some help in determining which dream is optimal for you to pursue at this time.

STAY WITH YOUR VISION

After you've done the visualization meditation, spend time with your dream. Because the next thing that typically happens with people is they start discounting it. They start putting limits on it. Money issues come up, along with the fears, the doubts, and limiting beliefs. It's both beneficial and effective to write these limitations down as they show up.

The limitations go something like this: you hear that voice in your head, or maybe it's your mom or your dad, your partner, a family member, saying: 'Oh, you'll never be able to do that', 'You're no good at that', 'That costs too much money', or 'There's no way you could ever reach that dream. You're not smart enough.'

When any of those things come up, write them down right away and acknowledge them as limiting beliefs.

In the *Unleash Your Free Spirit: Change Your Life* program, I will show you how to let go of these limiting beliefs and get them out of your way, once and for all.

ACCESSING YOUR GIFTS, TALENTS, SKILLS AND INTERESTS

Talent is defined as 'something that you have a natural ability for. Something you've always shown an aptitude for, or a flair for.' What we want to do now is to go back over your life and look at what makes you unique. What makes you... you? What gifts and talents did you come in with?

If you were to ask your mother or a sibling, it's the things they would remember that you were good at when you were young, although it could be something that showed up later in life as well. The latter was the case for me. I discovered in my 20s that I had a knack for songwriting. I had never written a song until I travelled to Australia, joined a rock 'n' roll cover band, and began singing my little ole heart out.

Spend a few minutes identifying ten gifts or talents that you have. Sometimes it's challenging for people to think of ten. If you have problems finding ten gifts or talents, start asking your family and friends.

Next I want you to look at your skills. These are things you have learned to do well through training, practice, and experience. So, while you have a gift or a talent for making people laugh, it becomes a skill when you've done stand-up comedy shows. When you've become good at doing stand-up performances, you can call yourself a comedian.

Skills usually show up on job requirements, things you would put on your resume, although they're not limited to jobs. You have skills that you use in your hobbies as well. Take into account everything, not just your job but other things you've done in your life that you are skilled at doing.

Finally, look at what I call your interests. Interests are the things that you have a tendency to do and choose to do regularly, or that you have a predisposition towards. Interests don't have to have anything to do with your gifts, talents, or skills. It could just mean that you've always had an interest in, say, gardening. But gardening may not relate necessarily to any of your gifts, talents and skills.

The purpose of this exercise is to get you to look at things from a number of angles. Your dream might be found in something you've never tried before but always had an interest in. To help you come up with your lists of gifts, talents, skills and interests, take a look at your life in periods of five to ten years. For your first ten years, think about what things you loved to do back then. Look at all of your gifts, talents, skills, and interests, and see if you can find patterns or common denominators in them. For me, I see a definite pattern throughout my life that involved teaching. Whatever it was I was doing, I always gravitated towards teaching people how to do it. It could have been a hobby like when I was making jewelry and then I started teaching classes on how to make it. Or the fact that I chose a public accounting job that allowed me to teach clients how to use tax software. When I look back through my life, being a teacher was a pattern all the way through. If I had a job that didn't involve teaching something, I wouldn't stick with it.

Look at all of these things and discover your patterns so that you can see how they fit into your dream, your vision, your goals. And don't forget to look at these lists and congratulate yourself for what an incredible, unique, talented, gifted being you are.

I have an artist client named Susan. She had been feeling overwhelmed and wasn't able to get anything going. She's not only a gifted artist but she also has a marketing and human resource background and worked in the corporate world as a teacher and motivator for many years. She's now close to 60 and she has all these ideas of things she still wants to do. But she just can't get started on any of them. So, I had her go back to the beginning and write down everything that was taking up her time; everything she did in a day, week, month, and year. During this process, she realized she had an amazing number of art classes that she teaches and/or had taught over the years. She'd actually forgotten some of them until she did this exercise. She saw how many skills, talents and gifts she had that were setting her up to move right into the next stage of her life. And she could see the flow in her life in all these amazing things that she's done.

By the time she got to the Dream Discovery step, she already had a clear picture of what she wanted to do. All she had to do was identify the tasks she needed to complete in order to create her dream job of teaching art to larger audiences through online programs, and then to find someone to help her with the things she doesn't do well so she could focus on her painting and creating the materials for her courses.

10
UNLEASH YOUR FREE SPIRIT IN EIGHT WEEKS

I've already walked you through some of the foundational principles for what it takes to get yourself out of career burnout and finally start living the life you want. These principles are what make up the *Change Your Life* eight-week course, which is a part of my *Unleash Your Free Spirit* online training program. Together, we're going to change your life, one step at a time.

WEEK ONE: LIFE, THE BIG PICTURE

In week one you will set your intention for what you want to do and identify all the things that have stopped you from doing it. These two critical steps are so simple that they are often ignored, so don't be fooled by their simplicity. They both must be done in order to effect the changes you want to make.

SETTING YOUR INTENTIONS

The first step is setting your intention for creating your dream life. What is it you want to achieve from this program? What is the change you want to make in your life?

Here's a short but sweet meditation exercise that you can use when setting your intention:

1. Close your eyes.
2. Be present in the moment. Let go all worries about the future and concerns about the past.
3. Focus on what you want. Solidify it in your mind.
4. Take slow, deep, cleansing breaths.
5. Set your intention.
6. Write it down.

For someone unhappy in their career and contemplating a career change but not sure what they want to do yet, the intention might be as simple as wanting to discover what it is they want to do. For someone who already knows what they want to do, their intention may be to clear their blocks and remove whatever is in the way of them moving forward, then taking the action steps to achieve their dreams, their goals, and their passion. The key is to write it down and even display it somewhere where you will see it. It's a constant reminder of what you want to do.

The second step in the first week is to create the space for the change that you want to make. Identify all the things you already have that fill up – and overfill – your schedule. Put them into three categories:

1. Activities that you can't let go – i.e. work, sleep, meals, time needed to get ready in the morning and at night, etc.
2. Activities that you'd rather not let go – exercise, family time, social activities.
3. Activities that you can let go. For instance, maybe you spend 2 hours a night watching TV. What if you take one of those hours and use it to start moving towards your dreams? That would give you seven extra hours a week.

You're going to have to let something go to create the space for the changes you want to make. That's the key to doing it. If you set your intention but don't make room for it, there's no point in going forward.

WEEKS TWO AND THREE: IN THE FLOW

In week two I ask you to forget about what it is that you want to change for a moment and go back through your life to rediscover what you're good at and what you love to do. The reason I take you away from focusing on your dream at this point is because you might have preconceived notions and you may be missing something that will be key to accomplishing your dreams. This process reminds you, 'Hey, you know what? Throughout my life,

I've always loved teaching, or helping others, or working with animals, or being in nature.' This is when you were in the flow. Take me, for instance. I always loved helping people make changes. That's my passion. So, when I find I'm going a little off course or I'm hitting some roadblocks, I remind myself how I feel when I help people make changes. That gets me back on track moving forward with my dreams and goals.

This process helps you remember the feeling of being in the flow, when you were doing something that you loved. For example, when you were pushing your body beyond its limits, or when you were working with wounded animals, or saving wild horses.

Flow is not about an elusive one-time thing. When you can get to the point where you're in the flow all the time, then you're in that state the Buddhists refer to as being 'calm in the midst of chaos'. Chaos can be happening all around you but it doesn't affect you. You remain in a place of peace and contentment. Of course, you don't do this overnight. It takes a lot of practice. To begin, you must first remember what it's like to be in the flow so you know when you aren't in the flow you can take action to get yourself back into it.

In week three we do a free-flow exercise to create a 'bucket list' of all the things you don't want to keep doing. Don't think too much about it. Just start writing down everything as it comes. Write down all the things in your past that didn't work using the following categories: work, family, social, personal, and money/financial. Include everything – past jobs, family issues, physical body issues, living arrangements with roommates that didn't work out, you name it. Watch for patterns or common denominators and observe when those things are still happening today. Once you are aware of them, you can choose to change the patterns.

WEEK FOUR: DREAM DISCOVERY

It's time to think big. This Dream Discovery phase is the time to let go of everything – all your limitations, all your money constraints, everything. Just let them go. It's also a time to acknowledge that you might have fear around your dream. Maybe you've tried before and it hasn't worked. Perhaps you've done a vision board but your dreams didn't come true. Don't let that stop you. Open yourself up. What do you want to do? What do you want your life to look like? As mentioned previously, go to the Additional Resources section in this book and you will find the link to the audio session where I will guide you through the Dream Discovery meditation.

WEEK FIVE: BREAKING DOWN LIMITING BELIEFS

Dream Discovery is like planting a bunch of seeds in your subconscious mind. In this next step, we talk about limiting beliefs that stand in the way of your dream. Limiting beliefs are like uncovering the seeds and saying, 'Why aren't you growing yet?' You kill the dream before it ever has a chance to take root. Limiting beliefs have no place in your dream life.

In the previous step, you identified your dreams, your goals, and your vision. You've got this wonderful feeling and you now feel excited about the future. You know you can make your dream come true! Then a couple weeks go by and you lose momentum. After more time, you've completely forgotten about your dream. The question is why. Why do we do that?

This step starts with addressing the ego. I'm defining ego here as the part of us that makes us unique. But it's also the part that protects us and thinks it needs to keep us safe. For this reason, the ego sometimes listens to the fear to avoid what it thinks will hurt us. For example, the ego may resist changes that put us in the public spotlight because of fears of being rejected, ridiculed, or even bullied.

The problem is that keeping us safe and protected is not allowing us to really live our lives. When it comes to reaching for our dreams, that's where we want to work with the ego to keep moving through the fears so we can find a balance between staying safe and moving forward.

Achieving a dream is not easy. If it was easy, you would have done it by now. It's important not to beat yourself up. Realize that working hard for something is just a part of life on this planet. Working through the limiting beliefs, moving and pushing beyond our fears and doubts, is what we're here to do. That's the challenge and that's where life comes alive. That's where *you* come alive. And that's when achieving those dreams finally becomes possible.

It doesn't mean that you ever finish working on your limiting beliefs, but every time you get over one more obstacle, you get to a new level of letting go of some limiting belief. It's magical every time you do it.

WEEK SIX: ACCESSING YOUR GIFTS AND TALENTS

In week six, we remind ourselves of all the things we're good at, why we have these dreams, and how we can achieve them.

I have clients who have said to me, 'I don't know what I've done in my life. I don't know what I'm good at.' They can be sitting there at the age of 55 not remembering any of their past talents or skills or interests that they have acquired over their lifetimes.

It's amazing how we can forget all of that. But we do. In particular, when you're looking at changing to a new career, that's where it comes up. It's that limiting belief that says, 'I could never change and do something new. I don't know anything else besides nursing. I don't know anything else besides painting.' But odds are you do. I want to work with you to help you remember that you have many skills, gifts, talents, and interests and no matter what you want do to in your life, you can take what you know and apply it to create a new and magical life.

WEEK SEVEN: LAY OUT YOUR PLAN

Week seven is where the rubber hits the road. So far you've been giving your dream a tune-up, priming the pump, making sure it's road ready. Now you are ready to make it happen. But first you need to chart your course, look at the map, draw a line from where you are to your destination, and lay out your plan to get there. It's goal setting 101 with a few twists and turns. I want you to lay it all out from the big goals down to the baby steps. What do you have to do to achieve your dream: the phone calls, the research, things you can start doing now?

But before you do that, pull out your dream and look at it again. See if the dream has already started to change because of your limiting beliefs. We want to get back to the full dream and not limit it. There is no room for 'I would do it, but…'.

Now look at your dream from the perspective of your gifts, talents, skills, and interests. Make sure your dream is as big as it can be including all of the unique qualities that are you, the talents that you've forgotten you have, and the skills you've developed that you seem to discard as 'nothing really'.

What has changed in the dream since you did the meditation? For example, maybe your dream was to have your own company become a seven-figure operation in five years, but now two weeks later you've forgotten that you were thinking seven figures. Maybe you've changed your mind because it seems impossible. Perhaps you've started getting into the trees and lost sight of the entire forest. It took only two weeks to downgrade your dream from a premium package to the basic package. It's so important to keep remembering your big vision and to remember the feeling you had when you first envisioned your dream.

Now write down where you want to be ten years from now. Then bring it back to five years. Then bring it down to one year, then six months, and eventually to one month, next week, and tomorrow.

BREAKING IT DOWN INTO BABY STEPS EXERCISE

Once you get the one-year plan down to the one-month plan, it's time to identify the detailed tasks that need to be done. To begin, identify up to 20 items that are important for you to do in the next six months. Pick six that are high priority to get started in the next month. Then break each of these six items down into baby steps.

It might be as simple as you need to do some online research on how to set up a business. Maybe another step is to do a name search for your new business. If you break them down into baby steps, the process is not overwhelming and you can do it. Start doing one or two each day. Get your list going!

ACTION PLANNING SHEET

I've created an action planning sheet to help you lay out your plan. It will guide you to identify the six critical steps you need to take in the month and break them down into the baby steps you can take this week to get you started on finally making the changes in your life that you have dreamed about for years. Simply go to the Additional Resources page of this book, find the link, print it out and start to check items off of your to-do list. Nothing feels better than to make that check mark each time you complete something!

WEEK 8: COACHING – KEEP THE MOMENTUM

The final step is moving forward. How do you keep the momentum going now that you have gotten this far? How do you keep going so that you get to your one-year, five-year and ten-year goals? One of the big things I do is encourage people to find a coach. Surround yourself with a support team, with cheerleaders. They will help you keep going when you get off track, when you hit external obstacles that you can't seem to get around, and when you discover fears and limiting beliefs that are doing their best to sabotage you.

For me, coaching was invaluable. It wasn't until I came back after years of traveling that I discovered I had done as much as I could by myself and it was time to get some support. I'd always been on a path of self-development and self-improvement but I was no longer making progress like I had when I was in my 20s and 30s. I needed help and feedback to see why I kept having the same challenges show up. I had relationship challenges where I always seemed to butt heads with bosses or people I worked with. The way I would resolve them in the past was to leave the organization. In addition, I had my lifelong fear of looking foolish in front of people, which kept me from stepping out. It wasn't until I had my first coach that I decided to stay and actually face the things that I didn't like looking at in myself and work through them. Coaching helped me immeasurably and it can help you, too.

DISCOVER YOURSELF – MAKE THE CALL

Coaching is one of *the most* beneficial, yet overlooked, discounted and ignored, gifts you can give yourself. Treat yourself to a Discovery Call with me and keep the momentum going. I've provided room in my schedule to talk to you one on one. I will help you discover the missing link for you that is keeping you from making the changes that you want to make.

Don't stop now! Today is the day to give the rest of your life a new and exciting outlook. Go to the Additional Resources section for the link to a questionnaire where I ask you to tell me a little bit about yourself and schedule your session.

YOUR PERSONAL BOARD OF DIRECTORS

You've got a dream, you've got a plan, and you're getting help. Now it's time to think about setting up a board of directors for YOU. Call it your board of directors, your personal team, or whatever you want to call it. It's about accountability, to help make sure you are staying on track and maintaining momentum. On your board of directors will be your coaches, your mentors, and other people who keep you focused. You choose them and ask them for help. They could include people who inspire you or have a certain skill set that you don't have. It's important to set it up and equally important to take it seriously. Surround yourself with people who know more than you do so that you are always learning, always challenging yourself, and always moving forward.

CONCLUSION

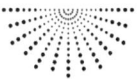

You've now learned about my eight-week course *Change Your Life* from my *Unleash Your Free Spirit* online learning program. I've shared much with you on what limits us in achieving our goals and how we can discover and create our dream lives.

But it is not the end. Far from it. It is important to remember that this is an ongoing process. You never stop. After you graduate, you keep moving on to the next chapter of your life. You never officially get to the end. And you celebrate along the way.

The challenge is to keep the momentum up – to keep reaching for your dreams. Don't let life get in the way. As with anything, you have to keep working at it.

Author and motivational speaker Zig Ziglar said, "People often say that motivation doesn't last. Well, neither does bathing. That's why we recommend it daily." Work at achieving your dreams just like you work at any good relationship, whether it's a marriage or business partnership. It can be challenging. It can be hard. But you must set the intention to work at it and keep at it.

Along with the motivation and keeping your momentum, you need to have perseverance, commitment, determination, and courage. As you're working through the program, I recommend putting those words up on your mirror or getting to the point where they are in your head all the time. As any Olympic athlete might tell you, you cannot achieve your dreams without perseverance, commitment, determination, and courage.

I recently heard an interview with a man who climbed Mount Everest. He'd tried a couple years previously and didn't make it, so he returned to try again. During the interview he said with a kind of awe that he'd discovered something else about perseverance. The group had been waiting at base camp to climb and ended up having to wait longer than they'd expected. So, it became a week, and then it became almost two weeks before they could go. They waited and waited. And he said he realized that patience is another form of perseverance.

Patience is a 'virtue' that we forget about when we are trying to achieve our big dreams and goals. Remember, they don't just happen immediately. There are no overnight successes. Those people who are called overnight successes typically laugh or shake their heads because nobody knows how long each one worked at it to become an 'overnight success'.

Our schools teach the three Rs: reading, writing, and 'rithmetic. But they don't teach the importance of perseverance, commitment, determination, and courage. In this modern life, it is common for us all to become impatient, frustrated, and then we just quit.

Don't quit.

Remember these attributes. When things get tough tell yourself, 'I'm not giving up. I'm going to hang on to this and I'm determined to make it work. I might not be doing it the right way right now, and people might be looking at me wondering what the heck I am doing, but I don't care. I'm going to make it. I'm determined and I'm not going to let anything or anyone stop me.'

Don't ever forget there is only one you. You are unique. There are more than seven billion people on the planet now and everyone has their own way of doing things and their own skills, gifts and talents. While you can gain a great deal of information from everything you read and hear from other people, you have to start to trust in your own process and what works for you.

Buddhists say if you're going to climb a mountain there are many paths to the top. The key is to pick one. So, pick *your* path and stick with it. Otherwise you're just walking around the base of the mountain and you won't make any progress. Follow your heart, your own path, and let go of limitations and fears. Then one day, not only will you have achieved your dreams, you will have become a free-spirited woman and a role-model for generations to come.

ADDITIONAL RESOURCES

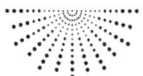

All of the additional resources listed below can be found on the following website: www.thefreespirit-project.org/and-now-its-your-turn/additional-resources

FREE SPIRIT MANTRA CARD

This includes the seven limiting beliefs and their opposite self-affirming beliefs. Laminate it and keep it with you at all times.

DREAM DISCOVERY VISUALIZATION AUDIO RECORDING

You will be guided through a meditation that will help you discover and clearly define your dream.

CLARITY ON THE DREAM DISCOVERY PROCESS VIDEOS

What if I have more than one dream? This video will help you if you have questions or concerns about the Dream Discovery process, if you have more than one dream, or you want some help in determining which dream is optimal for you to pursue at this time.

What if I am not sure what dream I want to pursue? What if I can't make up my mind? What if I don't even have a dream yet? This video will help you if you have questions or concerns about the Dream Discovery process and need ideas about how to approach this manifestation if you want some help in determining which dream is optimal for you to pursue at this time.

ACTION PLANNING SHEET

This helps you lay out your plan, identify the six critical steps you need to take in the next month, and break them down into the baby steps you can take this week to get you started on finally making the changes in your life that you have dreamed about for years. Print this out and start to check items off of your to-do list. Nothing feels better than to make that check mark each time you complete something!

DISCOVERY CALL

Treat yourself to a Discovery Call with me and keep the momentum going. I've provided room in my schedule to talk to you one on one. I will help you discover the missing link for you that is keeping you from making the changes that you want to make. Don't stop now! Today is the day to give the rest of your life a new and exciting outlook. Fill out the questionnaire where I ask you to tell me a little bit about yourself and schedule your session. Do it now before your limiting beliefs get the better of you!

ABOUT THE AUTHOR

Martha Moore is a transformational life coach known for her unique style of no-nonsense and insightful guidance. She started on her path almost 30 years ago, receiving her MBA and practicing as a CPA for several years before leaving a successful career behind to follow her heart by travelling the world. She worked her way around Australia for two years, spent three months on an African safari, travelled alone through the Middle East and volunteered for a year in India. After years of international travel and study, she settled in Colorado to become a life coach, teacher, author, and mentor. For the past 15 years, she has devoted her life to helping others discover the joy of following their own hearts and uncovering the courage, strength and passion that is within. In October 2014, The Free Spirit Project was born out of the desire to share this feeling with the world. The project is a place for free spirits to gather, learn, share, laugh, and to move through fears and blocks and truly live life to its fullest – to fly free.

END NOTES

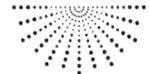

Traits of a Free Spirited Woman, from *Mind, Body, Green*, April 14 2017 https://www.mindbodygreen.com/0-29738/7-traits-of-free-spirited-women.html

www.ingramcontent.com/pod-product-compliance
Lightning Source LLC
Chambersburg PA
CBHW060349190426
43201CB00043B/1892

9 780995 934672